SOLD!

OVERTHROWING THE STATUS QUO IN THE CAR BUSINESS

SETH DAVIS
CREATOR OF THE FULL CIRCLE SALES APPROACH

ISBN: 978-1-4834-4571-7 (sc)
ISBN: 978-1-4834-4570-0 (e)

Because of the dynamic nature of the Internet, any web addresses or links contained in
this book may have changed since publication and may no longer be valid. The views
expressed in this work are solely those of the author and do not necessarily reflect the
views of the publisher, and the publisher hereby disclaims any responsibility for them.

Any people depicted in stock imagery provided by Thinkstock are models,
and such images are being used for illustrative purposes only.
Certain stock imagery © Thinkstock.

Lulu Publishing Services rev. date: 02/03/2016

Dedicated to my amazing, goofy, loving kids, who serve as a constant reminder that I'll always be 14 years old at heart. I love you two more than anything in this world. You keep me motivated and inspired every day. I will leave a legacy for the two of you that you will always be proud of.
-Dad

Status Quo, You Know, Is Latin
For "The Mess We're In"
-Ronald Reagan

**This Book Is An Unapologetic Declaration
Of War On The Status Quo.**

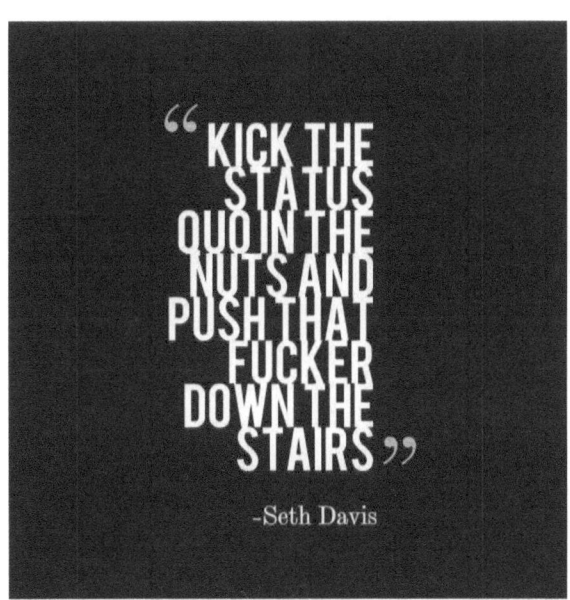

CONTENTS

INTRODUCTION

When I was 20 years old, I stopped at a local Car Dealership to check out a used car that had caught my eye. A Salesperson named Karl came out to greet me. Karl proceeded to show me the vehicle in question, and then he began to ask me some qualifying questions. "Do you have a trade-in?" Yes, I do, I replied. "How many miles are on it?" I answered Karl. Then he asked, "what are you looking to get out of it?" I'd like to get ten thousand for it, I replied. Karl immediately gave me a look as if I had just grabbed his wife's ass, "what are you on drugs?"

I was a pretty introverted, laid back kid. But, I had a hot temper. Karl doesn't know how close he came to getting punched in the face on that Summer afternoon. However, I got into my car and left. I certainly wasn't about to put a nickel in that guy's pocket. He had just cost himself a Car Deal with a few poorly chosen words. Karl exemplified everything that was wrong with the Car Business. It is guys like him who have given Automotive Salespeople a bad stigma for decades and continue to until this very day.

A couple of months later, I managed to land a job selling cars at a local Dealership. Yes, the very same Dealership. Karl did not remember me, but I certainly remembered Karl, and I had a bone to pick. (No, I did not punch Karl in the face)

The way that this Dealership taught me to approach the sale was the same run of the mill "Old School, Always Be Closing" sales approach that has been prevalent in the Car Business for decades. Get the Customer to know you, like you, and trust you. *No shit*. Then, when you get the Customer back to your desk, turn up the heat, and turn up the pressure, in an effort to get the Customer to sign on the dotted line right here, right now! That was the part of the process that seemed to be counterproductive to me. I felt confident that I could do better.

2002 was my first full year at that Dealership, my first full year in the Car Business. Not only did I outsell Karl, that "Salesperson" who had pissed me off the Summer before. I also outsold everybody else in the Dealership, including all of the Veterans who had sold cars there for years. They were pissed. It didn't make sense to them how this introverted, socially awkward shy kid could outsell all of them. I didn't even take that many Fresh Customers! They were perplexed. I, on the other hand, was happy as a clam. And, I had a pocket full of Cash.

I believe that my introversion played a big role in my success in the Car Business. I hated taking Fresh Customers, so I had to find a way to capitalize on a higher percentage of the people that I DID speak to. Fortunately for you, that's exactly what I did. And now, I'm going to teach you the exact same methods in this book. If a goofy fucker like me can do it, so can you.

Throughout my thirteen years in the Car Business, I would go on to repeatedly accomplish seemingly impossible feats. I was able to maintain a 60% plus Closing Ratio, some of the highest Customer Satisfaction Scores in the Region, and at times, I had more Repeat and Referral Business than I could handle. My Sales were on Autopilot. If that sounds like a problem you'd like to have, you're in the right place. In 2005, I took a random Sales Phone Call that led to 505 Car Deals and over $212,000 in Commissions.

By the time I was 23, I had a beautiful home, awesome cars, and a gorgeous Girlfriend, who would later become my Wife. My life was amazing; I was on cloud nine...

Now I know why the divorce rate is so high. It didn't take long before things started to go south between the Wife and myself. In 2011, we went through a divorce. It was by far the most anguish that I had ever experienced. In addition to the emotional grief, I also lost my home, and nearly everything else that I had worked so hard for. It sucked. I then went on an out of control drinking binge that lasted over a year. Not the brightest idea.

In 2013, I woke up in the middle of the night with completely numb arms, and I was having difficulty breathing. I was certain that I would pass out and die. I was having heart attack/stroke like symptoms. Not a pleasant feeling. What the hell is this! I had been healthy my entire life. These attacks happened ten or fifteen times during the next month or so, even once while I was driving 75 miles per hour down the highway! After repeated visits to the Hospital, and a battery of tests, including one that determined that I had an abnormality on my pituitary gland.

I have a brain tumor?? Are you freaking kidding me!? (That turned out to be false, thank God) My Family Doctor was finally able to accurately diagnose the problem. He put me on medication, and I haven't had an episode since. Wow.

In 2014, I made the decision to leave the Car Business. I desired a Monday through Friday, 9-5 schedule that would afford me more time to spend with my beautiful kids. Spending more time with them was very important to me. So, I landed a job doing Outside Sales for a local Company. This is where things get interesting...

It just so happens that roughly 110 of my Accounts were New and Used Car Dealerships. Even though I was no longer in the Car Business, I was still in and out of Car Dealerships five days a week. I was still in my element. I began to notice almost right away that some of these Dealerships were thriving while others were struggling to stay afloat. At first, it didn't make any sense to me. Some of these Dealerships were in very close proximity to each other. They all had decent products and fair prices, what the hell was going on here? Now I was curious what was causing the disparity...

I began to pay close attention to the interaction between the Salespeople and their Customers. Bingo! The approach to the sale was very different between the Dealerships that were thriving, and the Dealerships that were floundering. Then it struck me! One of the biggest things that I missed about being in the Car Business was coaching and mentoring other Salespeople! I had coached hundreds of Salespeople over the years who were eager to learn my bass-ackwards approach to the sale that had made me a standout during my tenure in the Car Business. Watching them succeed was an awesome feeling. I loved it, and I missed it.

Not long after, I purchased a webcam and began making informative videos for Automotive Sales Professionals. They were plastered all over the Internet, and it didn't take long for me to develop a following. My approach to the sale flew in the face of the status quo. I vehemently challenged the "Old School" sales approach that had been the standard for so many years, and Salespeople all over the World began to take notice. It quickly became crystal clear that I was onto something big.

Always one to enjoy a challenge, I decided to overthrow the status quo. It took months to really break down and reverse engineer the methods that I had used throughout my time in the Car Business to accomplish the things that I was able to accomplish. When the dust settled, "The Full Circle Sales Approach" was born.

I developed a Business Entity, purchased a camera, a backdrop, studio lighting, and began shooting The Full Circle Sales Approach Online Course. My first ever Online Course was loaded with great content, but it was boring as hell. It was painful to watch. I was not yet comfortable on camera and didn't utilize my goofy ass sense of humor that had made me so popular with my coworkers and Customers alike. So, I went back to the drawing board and reshot the entire Course. This time, I got it right. Better content, more engaging, and pretty damn humorous.

The concept behind The Full Circle Sales Approach is very simple. However, the execution requires that you take very specific steps to maximize the effectiveness of this approach. This book, as well as the Online Course, are designed to guide you, in detail, along every step in the Sales Process. Putting these principles into Action will help you dramatically increase your Closing Ratio, sell more cars, and make more Money. And, I will NEVER ask you to take any more Fresh Customers than you already do. You are just going to capitalize on a higher percentage of the Customers that you already encounter.

The way that the average Consumer shops for vehicles has changed dramatically since I started in the Car Business back in 2001. Customers now have access to a helluva lot more information than they did back then. The Information Age has very much leveled the playing field. Therefore, Customers are less and less willing to tolerate pushy Salespeople, because they know that they have other options.

Did you know that Lending Institutions all over the Country are creating "Car Buying" programs for their Members to circumvent the traditional car shopping process? These Lending Institutions do the leg work for their Members to alleviate the anxiety that seems to be synonymous with car shopping. High-pressure sales approaches have done much more damage than good. You know it's time for a change when Banks and Credit Unions are capitalizing on the fact that the General Public dreads car shopping that much. This is the stigma that the "Old School" approach to the sale has so kindly left for you.

The vast majority of Car Dealerships are trying to combine New School Marketing with the Old School/High-Pressure/Always Be Closing Approach To The Sale. There is no synergy. It doesn't make sense to spend a fortune to get Potential Customers through the door if you're just piss away 75% of them. It's well past time for a change. It isn't 1995 anymore.

Get your highlighter out! If you spot something in this book that really resonates with you, highlight it, bookmark it, or staple it to your forehead. (Please don't literally staple anything to your forehead) I would like to take this time to point out that no foreheads, human or otherwise, were harmed during the creation of this book.

Thank you so much for checking this book out! If you read it with an open mind, you will not be disappointed. If you put this sales approach into Action, I will not be held responsible for the destruction of your wallet as a result of the sudden influx of Cash thrust into said wallet. Enjoy! -Seth Davis

For More Information About The Full Circle
Sales Approach Online Course, Visit
www.fullcirclesalesapproach.com

CHAPTER 1

What Is The Full Circle Sales Approach?

*You Can Have Everything In Life You
Want, If You Will Just Help Enough
Other People Get What They Want*
-Zig Ziglar

Imagine what your life will look like with a 50% Closing Ratio. Take a few moments, and imagine giving yourself a $20,000 or $25,000 a year pay raise. What does your standard of living look like? How much better are you able to provide for your Family? What kind of car is parked in your driveway? What does your home look like? This is very powerful stuff. *And remember, this is all possible without taking any more Fresh Customers than you already do.*

The very first goal that I have for you is a <u>50% Closing Ratio</u>.

Let's dig a little deeper, here. Let's say you already talk to 40 Customers a month, between Fresh Customers, Repeat Business, and Referrals. And, you currently have a 30% Closing Ratio. The average Automotive Salesperson in the U.S. makes $250 per Car Deal. Below, you will see the effects of simply increasing your Closing Ratio, based on speaking to 40 Customers a month.

30% Closing Ratio = 12 Car Deals Per Month = 144 Car Deals Per Year = $36,000 Per Year

40% Closing Ratio = 16 Car Deals Per Month = 192 Car Deals Per Year = $48,000 Per Year

50% Closing Ratio = 20 Car Deals Per Month = 240 Car Deals Per Year = $60,000 Per Year

*These are very conservative estimates based on National Averages and do not factor in Volume Bonuses, Spins, Fast Start Bonuses, Etc. If you sold 240 Cars at my Former Dealership, you'd make $120,000 Plus.

It's not too difficult to see the benefits of simply increasing your Closing Ratio. You don't need to take 200 Fresh Customers a month to sell a shit load of cars and make a shit load of Money. It just isn't necessary. If you are holding this book in your hands, you are on the right track. Put these Principles into Action, and don't look back.

First, let's state the obvious, it's important that you have a quality product at a fair price. Both of these things are *subjective*. What one Customer perceives as a quality product, the next Customer who walks into your showroom might perceive as a piece of crap. What one Customer perceives as a fair price, might be perceived as highway robbery to the next Customer. **Perception Is Reality. The more you understand and embrace this quote, the more you will be able to capitalize on it for the rest of your Sales Career.**

The foundation for The Full Circle Sales Approach is "The Law Reciprocity." The Law Of Reciprocity has been proven time and time again in Social Psychology and Business, and it says that when someone does something nice for you, you will have a deep-rooted psychological urge to do something nice in return. Some of the largest industries on the planet have been capitalizing on this Law for decades. The Car

Business as a whole has not caught up, yet. Which means you have a golden opportunity to get way out ahead of the curve, and get way out ahead of your competition *now* before they catch on.

Here's why it's so effective in the Car Business; *Because Almost Nobody Else Does It. What makes you stand out from your competition, makes you outstanding to your Customer.* Do You want to outsell your competition? Don't do the same shit that they do. Stand out. *See the status quo for what it really is, a nemesis that is robbing you of <u>Car Deals</u> and <u>Money</u> every single month! Kick the status quo in the nuts and push that fucker down the stairs! Now is your time to shine.*

If you have a quality product at a fair price, the rest is up to <u>you</u>, the Salesperson. Referring to the quote at the beginning of this Chapter; You can have all the Car Deals and make all the Money you want if you'll just help enough Customers get what they want -a quality product at a fair price AND a great Buying Experience.

This is how you capitalize on The Full Circle Sales Approach and The Law Of Reciprocity in a sales environment; When you give every Customer an outstanding Buying Experience that they truly enjoy, when it comes time to ask for the sale, they will feel a deep-rooted psychological urge to *reciprocate* by saying yes, I'll take it! Let's write it up! This is music to our ears as Sales Professionals. Amirite? Get used to hearing it. A lot.

So, you see, in concept, The Full Circle Sales Approach is very simple. You might be thinking to yourself "Dude, I totally already do that shit, my Customers freakin' love me." There's a strong chance that you already do a lot of the things discussed in this book. However, *if you currently have a 25% or 30% Closing Ratio, something is missing that is Costing you Car Deals and Costing you Money.* As you read through this book, you will probably discover what it is that's missing. It will smack you upside the head. Then, when you put what you've discovered into Action, your Closing Ratio will suddenly go up, you'll sell more cars, and you'll make more Money.

How is The Full Circle Sales Approach different from the "Old School, Always Be Closing" sales approach that's been a staple in the Car Business for decades? And why is it more effective? Over the years, I've had thousands of Customers tell me that they hate car shopping. Why is this so common? Is it because they really don't want to trade their rusted out old jalopy for a shiny new car? Of course not. The general public dreads the car shopping process because so many Salespeople make it unpleasant and uncomfortable. As a result of these repeated unpleasant experiences with other Salespeople in the past, they walk onto your lot with a level of anxiety and cynicism. They have the perception that they have to fight with you, the Salesperson, to get a good deal on their new car. Using The Full Circle Sales Approach, you change that perception. ***You will give your Customer the perception that you are on their team, that you are their advocate, and that you are going to fight for them, not with them.***

Take a wild guess what happens when your Customer sees you fighting *for* them instead of *with* them? Your Closing Ratio goes up, you sell more cars, and you make more Money. Ask yourself, who would you rather buy a car from, the Salesperson who backs you into a corner and fights with you to sign on the dotted line? Or, the Salesperson who aligns their interests with yours, and goes to battle on your behalf? I feel dumber after just asking that question. You are much more likely to sell a car to a Customer who ***wants*** to do business with you vs. a Customer who you try to force into doing business with you.

Using this approach to the sale, at no point are you going to use high-pressure tactics, at no point are you going to back your Customer into a corner, and at no point are you going to intentionally make your Customer feel uncomfortable. You will give every Customer an amazing Buying Experience, and subsequently reap the benefits. You will fight tooth and nail for every Car Deal, regardless of what you are going to make on it. No more working for free.

"50% of something is better than 100% of nothing." The first time I heard that quote, I think my head hit the ceiling. It perfectly coincided with what I had been preaching for over a decade! One of the biggest lessons that I learned very early in my Career in the Car Business was that my ticket to success is this Business was *Volume*. Once I discovered this, I fought like a rabid Pit Bull for every single Car Deal. I wanted the Car Deals that I was going to make $100 on just as much as I wanted the Car Deals that I was going to make $500 on. ***Your ticket to financial success in the Car Business is VOLUME. Never forget this. Don't spend three or four hours with a Customer without making any Money.***

Let's make something clear before we move forward; using this approach *does not* necessitate that you be a "giveaway artist." My coworkers used to bust my balls all the time for being a giveaway artist, probably because I fought so hard for *every* Car Deal. However, my average earnings were just over $420 per Car Deal. Often, your Customer will pay you *more* than your competition because you provided them with such a great Buying Experience, and because they know your competition will probably put them through the all too common Car Sales "gauntlet."

Let's talk goal setting for a few moments. My method of goal setting is a bit different than the traditional method of goal setting in the Car Business. It's up to you to decide how many cars you want to sell this month or this year. We are going to take your goal setting one step further. You are going to discover your "why." Why do you want to sell more cars and make more Money? There must be a motive or motives behind that desire. What are they? Maybe you want a new car? A new boat? Perhaps you want to build a new home? Maybe you'd like to provide a better life for your Family? Maybe you want to become a Sales Manager at some point? Take some time right now, and discover your why(s). We all have goals, dreams, and ambitions. What are yours?

Once you've discovered your why or why's, write them down in detail. These are your new goals. These are what you will keep your eyes on as you move forward this month, and this year. The next step is to create a deadline for each written goal. Create a deadline that you believe is realistic, but you need to challenge yourself. Push yourself. Next, create a visual for each written goal. This is easier to do if the goal is something material. Rip a picture out of a magazine, print a picture off of the internet, etc. Now, put them someplace where you will see them all the time.

"Seth, why am I doing all of this weird shit?"

Studies have shown over and over again that just the act of writing down your goals make you much more likely to achieve them. Creating a deadline challenges you to achieve your goal(s) sooner than later. And creating a visual that coincides with your written goal(s) serves to keep you motivated and inspired to reach that desired end result. Why does this work? Taking these three simple steps forces your subconscious mind into overdrive, so even when you aren't thinking about your goal(s) consciously, the wheels are still turning in your subconscious mind, trying to find the most efficient path to your desired end result. It works.

"Seth, how do you know that this method of goal setting works?"

When I was 23 years old, one of my older buddies had a Z06 Corvette. At that time, the Z06 was one of the baddest American Sports Cars on the road. He let me drive it a few times, and I was smitten. I decided that I had to have one. So, I wrote it down in detail and created a deadline. I already had pictures all over my house, so that part was covered. I can remember very vividly obsessing over this car while I was on the treadmill at the gym. I was picturing the car in my driveway. I was imagining driving it down the highway. Guess what happened next? Over the next few months, I sold a TON of cars and made a TON of Money. I found a good deal on exactly what I was looking for down in Georgia, struck up a deal right over the phone, and had my Torch Red Z06 shipped to Upstate New York. There is sat in my driveway. Pretty sure I spent more time in that car than I did in my house.

My First Corvette Circa 2004

I have experienced results like this on many occasions over the years, and I've seen many other people do the same thing. There's no question about whether or not this method of goal setting works. It just plain does. ***But, it does require that you take Action.*** We aren't done talking about goal setting just yet. I have a few goals for you, too. Three to be exact, pretty simple. You will want to write these down.

1. Bat .500

By the time you finish reading this book and put this Approach into Action, you will have at least a 50% Closing Ratio. If a socially awkward introvert can maintain these kind of numbers for thirteen years, I know you can!

2. Higher CSI Scores

This one is specifically for New Car Salespeople. One of the many benefits of using The Full Circle Sales Approach is higher Customer Satisfaction Scores. If you sell new cars, you know how important it is to get great CSI Scores. Consider it done!

3. Create Assets

Another byproduct of using this Sales Approach is creating Customers for life. These are people who will come to you repeatedly when they need vehicles in the future. Many of them will also send or bring you referrals. An Asset is something that makes you Money, an economic resource.

Once you have two or three thousand Assets out there in your Community who are coming back to you repeatedly for vehicles in the future and sending you or bringing you referrals, your job gets pretty damn easy. Your sales will be on autopilot at that point. *There is a caveat to creating a lot of Assets in your Community though, it requires that you stay employed at ONE Dealership.* I know so many Salespeople who bounce around from one Dealership to another. Some of your Loyal Customers might follow you around from Dealership to Dealership… but many of them won't. Especially if they are brand loyal. ***If you work for a Dealership that treats you well and pays you well, stay there. You'll thank me later.***

While we're on the subject of Assets, let's talk Assets vs. Liabilities for a moment. An Asset is something that *makes* you Money (Happy Customer); a Liability is something that *costs* you Money (Pissed Off Customer). Word of mouth is still our best source of advertisement, but it's no longer a one on one interaction. Your Happy Customer (Asset) will go home after picking up their shiny new car, take a picture of it with their smartphone, and plaster it all over Social Media, along with a message singing your praises. With a few simple keystrokes, they advertise for you to hundreds or even thousands of people, and it makes an impression on these people. Guess what the Pissed Off Customer (Liability) does after they leave your Dealership angry? In a fit of rage, they go home, jump on Social Media, and with a few simple keystrokes, talk shit about you and your Dealership. Instantly, this information goes out to hundreds or even thousands of people, and it makes an impression on these people.

It's not too difficult to see why you want to really maximize your Assets and really minimize your Liabilities. Listen, no matter how many hoops you jump through, there are certain people who will leave your Dealership pissed off. More often than not, because they think their trade is worth $20,000 when it's really worth $12,000. I get it. Been there, done that. But, using this Approach, you will truly minimize that from happening. The odds will tilt in your favor.

CHAPTER 2

Let's Make A Great First Impression

You Only Get One Chance To
Make A Great First Impression
-Unknown

Making a great first impression is so important in the Car Business. First, I want to make you aware of a couple of things that Customers really don't like, pitfalls that I see far too many Salespeople fall into so that you can avoid making those costly mistakes. Then, we'll discuss the best ways to make a great first impression, whether it be on your lot, in your showroom, or over the phone. Look, you wouldn't be a Sales Professional if you weren't likable and charismatic. And, the vast majority of Salespeople who I've worked with over the years also have a great sense of humor. You can capitalize on those attributes throughout the entire Buying Process, starting with that great first impression.

One thing that Customers *really don't like*; Being attacked the moment they step foot on your lot. Customers don't like feeling overwhelmed or smothered right out of the gate. I've been saying for years that I would love to implement a two-minute rule. This would give every lot Customer two minutes to exit their vehicle, and get a little comfortable on your lot *before* a Salesperson approaches them. Nobody's going to get pissed off that they had to wait two minutes before a Salesperson approached them. But, they are much more likely to be receptive if they are a little comfortable before that first interaction.

Another thing that makes a terrible first impression; A Salesperson who approaches the Customer with his hands in his pockets, shirt half untucked, dragging his feet, and when he reaches the Customer he stops and says "can I help ya?" This is *not* a good way to make a great first impression. If you have a habit of doing either one of the things discussed above, now would be a good time to stop doing those things. They are not helping your Career. Not even a little.

What is the best way to make a great first impression? For lot Customers; Approach them with a brisk pace, with ambition and enthusiasm, and when you reach them, hold out your hand and say "Hi! Welcome to ABC Motors, my name is Seth, and your name? (My fictitious Customer is named Susan.) Nice to meet you, Susan. What brings you in today?" Always shake the Customer's hand at that first introduction, and always hand them your Business Card right up front. (We'll discuss why it's important to hand every Fresh Customer your Business Card right up front in a moment.) Next, I would reach into my pocket, pull out something to write on, and write Susan's name down. Why? I've had a terrible memory my entire life, so writing their name down immediately was a necessity to avoid looking like a dumbass for forgetting their name after 10 seconds. If you have a photographic memory, I'm jealous, but you can skip that step.

Why is it important to hand every Fresh Customer your Business Card right up front? What if Susan has a terrible memory? Now, she has ready access to your name because it's right on your Business Card. Also, there's nothing worse than spending two or three hours with a Customer, who had to leave your Dealership suddenly for one reason or another, then realizing after they left that you never gave them your Business Card. Inevitably, they will come back a couple of days later to see you, but they can't remember your name because you never gave them your Business Card, and the next thing you know they're buying a car from one of your coworkers. Not cool. I've had this happen to me before, and it sucks. Start handing Fresh Customers your Business Card right up front.

What about the Customers who spot you approaching, so they turn and walk away? This used to drive me bananas, until I found a way around it. If a Customer started walking away the moment they spotted me exit my showroom, I would walk down a separate aisle, parallel to them, as if I didn't even see them. Then, at the last second, I would suddenly turn to them and say "I'm sorry, are you folks being taken care of?" This is a great, low-key opener for a Customer, who was clearly anxious about a Salesperson approaching them. Instead of chasing them down and smothering them, you are expressing concern about whether or not they are being taken care of. You will diffuse their anxiety in an instant. Excellent ice breaker.

Let's address the seemingly omnipresent elephant in the room, "just looking." Just looking is just a knee-jerk response that most of us are programmed to say whenever a Salesperson greets us. I've done it a thousand times, myself. Most of the time, just looking is just a little speed bump that you will get over. Never let just looking take the wind out of your sails. The objective should be to get the Customer to start asking you questions. Once they start asking questions, you've moved past just looking, and on to the next step in the process.

Here's how I used to get past just looking; "Ok, is there something specific that you're looking for? Perhaps I can point you in the right direction…" Often, the Customer would start asking me questions. Bingo! Now we were on to the next step in the process. Look, some Customers who say "just looking" *really* don't want to be bothered. Here's how I handled those Customers; "I understand, here's my card, my name is Seth, if you have any questions, I'll be right in the showroom, ok?" Then I would walk back to the showroom. However, what I would do next is important. I would keep an eye on them from the showroom. If they were still wandering my lot ten or fifteen minutes later, I'd approach them a second time. Now, I'm a familiar face. Upon my second approach, I'd say, "I see you guys are still here, I just wanted to touch base with you to see if you have any questions or if you'd like a brochure or anything before you leave." Chances are if they're still on my lot fifteen minutes after first contact, they probably have at least a couple questions. More often than not, they would start asking questions, and I had moved past just looking, and on to the next step in the process.

Customers who walk into your showroom typically have a slightly different mindset, most of them are walking into your showroom with a purpose. Maybe they spotted a car on your lot over the weekend that they'd like to test drive today. Or, perhaps they already have a good idea what kind of vehicle they want, so they walked in to grab a brochure. Your greeting with these people should be the same as your greeting with lot Customers. However, you don't want to make showroom Customers wait two minutes. You are much less likely to hear "just looking" from a Customer in your showroom.

A few simple yet powerful tips that I'd like to give you; Most people really like the sound of their own name, *and* get them to say the word "yes" to you periodically throughout the Buying Process. Combine the two, and you're setting yourself up to sell another car. Example; "Susan, that's a great color, isn't it?" Use your Customer's first name, and ask them questions that you know the answer is likely to be "yes" to. Using their first name makes you more likable to your Customer. It makes them more comfortable with you. Asking them "yes" questions throughout the Buying Process gets them used to saying "yes" to you. When they are used to saying "yes" to you, they are more likely to say "yes" when it comes time to ask for the Sale. Guys, don't go crazy with this, use some discretion. But, these subliminal Jedi mind tricks work. Use them.

Also, if you greet a Customer within the last ten days of the month or so, plant the seed in their mind that they will probably get a better deal if they purchase a vehicle from you before the end of the month. Here's how I used to word it; "Susan, you came it at just the right time! We just had a big meeting this morning, and we need to sell another thirty cars to hit our goal for the month. If you're looking for a great deal, your timing could not be better!" Everybody loves to save Money. Everybody wants to feel like he or she got a great deal. Planting this seed in your Customer's mind almost always persuades them to do business with you sooner than later. It works like magic, use this!

Now, let's talk about Phone Ups, my favorite subject! We've already established that you are likable and charismatic, and you most likely have a great sense of humor. You can capitalize on these things with Phone Customers just like you do with Customers who are standing three feet in front of you. Your Dealership probably has a specific greeting that they want you to use with your Phone Ups. The greeting that we used was an enthusiastic "New Cars, may I help you?" or "Used Cars, may I help you?" then we would go from there. They recorded our Phone Ups for a while. God that sucked.

I'm going to share a story with you about a random Phone Up that will hopefully inspire you, and show you the kind of thing that's possible using The Full Circle Sales Approach.

In February of 2005, our Operator paged us overhead "New Car Sales, line one." I happened to be the one who grabbed the phone first "New Cars, may I help you?" The guy on the other line was calling to get information on a vehicle for his Mother. His name was Gordon. At the time, we were supposed to use this canned phone script with every single Phone Customer. The problem was that this phone script was developed in the mid-1980's, long before the internet, smart phones, etc. It was outrageously outdated and incredibly ineffective. So, I refused to use it…and it's a good thing I did. Had I used this worthless phone script with Gordon, my response to one of his product questions would have been "Sir, I don't have that information in front of me, but I can have it for you by the time you arrive." Instead, I answered the Gordon's questions with enthusiasm. Then, he asked me for a price. This was *really* taboo at my Dealership. I could have gotten into major trouble, but I gave Gordon a great price right over the phone anyway. His Mother ended up not purchasing a vehicle at that time, although she purchased several over the next five or six years...

A few weeks went by, and one of Gordon's coworkers named Linda expressed interest in purchasing a new car. Linda just happened to want the same brand that I sold. When Gordon got wind of this, I was the first person that he thought of. You see, that day that I had my first interaction with Gordon over the phone a few weeks earlier, he had also called several other Dealerships looking for information and pricing. I was the *only* Salesperson who gave him the exact information that he had asked for. The other Salespeople that he had spoken to on that day had all given him a line of bullshit, probably similar to the line on that stupid ass phone script that I was supposed to use. I was the only Salesperson who had made a great impression on Gordon right over the phone.

He called me right away with Linda sitting in his office. "Seth, this is Gordon...we spoke on the phone a few weeks ago about a car for my Mother. I have a coworker sitting in my office; her name is Linda. Linda is interested in this specific vehicle. I need to know if you have it, and if you do, she's going to need a price." I didn't know the answers to these questions off the top of my head, so I told Gordon that I would check and get back to him right away. It just so happens that I had the exact car that Linda was looking for right in stock! And, I got her a good price. I called Gordon back with the good news. To my amazement, his response was "ok, she'll take it." Whaaaaat? I was a bit dumbfounded to say the least.

"Here's the problem," he said, "Linda has a crazy schedule, and we are calling from over seventy miles away. (I had no idea he was calling from that far away) She doesn't know when she's going to have time to come get the car." Immediately, a solution popped into my head! "Gordon, fax me her license, registration, and insurance card. I'll put the paperwork together, get the car ready, and deliver it right to Linda." This time, *he* was dumbfounded "you'll do that??" Absolutely, I replied. So, that's exactly what we did. My day off was the only day that would work for Linda, so I delivered her new car 73 miles to her on a Tuesday. *(We will talk about Time Management later in this book. I do not recommend that you work your day off unless you absolutely have no other choice.)*

What I didn't know about Gordon was that he was *very* influential in the Banking Industry. Not long after that first Car Deal with Linda, he had four or five people on his team who were all calling me with Referrals. They all had Customers who wanted my product and service. Nine years later, I had sold and delivered 505 vehicles, and made over $212,000 in commissions that had all stemmed from that random Phone Up back in February of 2005. Guess what would have happened had I used that dumb ass phone script that I was supposed to use with every Phone Up? Gordon is a very matter of fact, no nonsense kind of guy. He would have told me to go pound salt, and I would have missed out on 505 Car Deals and a lot of Money. Sometimes being a rule breaker pays off. A lot.

My Sales Managers used to say all the time "if you give your Customer a bunch of information over the phone, they have no reason to come to the Dealership." I vehemently disagree. If you give your Phone Customer information that intrigues them, you may very well strike a few hot buttons with them right over the phone. Add in a great phone personality, and the Customer will decide right over the phone whether or not they like you. *If you strike a few hot buttons right over the phone, and the Customer decides that they like you, they have all the more reason to come visit you in your showroom, not less reason.* My Sales Managers reasoning was an "Old School" mindset that really needs to go away. If I called a Dealership to ask a few product questions, and the Salesperson refused to answer my questions…, I'd be pissed. There's no way I'd step foot in that Dealership. And I believe that the majority of our Modern Society feels much the same way.

If you have a Customer on the phone who asks for information that you don't have immediate access to, do not just make shit up. Tell them you don't know off the top of your head, and that you'll get back to them right away. Be "Johnny On The Spot." Get the information, and call them back as fast as you can. Customers love that. It makes an awesome impression on them!

From here forward, use your likeability, your charisma, and your sense of humor to your advantage. Capitalize on your attributes. Make the Buying Process enjoyable. Make your Customers laugh! All of these things will make your Customer more comfortable with you. Don't pretend to be something that you're not. Most Customers can see right through an insincere Salesperson, unless that Salesperson happens to be an amazing actor. Customers don't want to do business with a Salesperson who is insincere.

Customers do want to do business with a Salesperson who makes it crystal clear right from first contact that they are on the Customer's team, that they are the Customer's advocate, and that they sincerely want to help the Customer find a vehicle that meets their wants, needs, and budget. This builds a huge amount of momentum. Add to that the perception that you are going to fight to get them the best deal possible, and you have yourself a winning combination.

Admittedly, I was not a big fan of Internet Leads. In my experience, the majority of Internet Customers sent in inquiries for one of three reasons. Either they wanted a unicorn vehicle that didn't exist, they were getting pricing from several different Dealerships to keep their local Dealership honest, or they wanted to see if we could get them approved for a Car Loan because they hadn't paid a bill since the last time the Yankees won the Super Bowl. My Closing Ratio with Internet Customers sucked. Hopefully, you have better luck with them than I did.

You now have a great understanding of how to make a great first impression, and why it's so important to do so. Get this part right, and most of the time the next step will fall into place!

18

CHAPTER 3

Walk Around And Test Drive

People Don't Buy For Logical Reasons.
They Buy For Emotional Reasons.
-Zig Ziglar

The walk around and test drives are your golden opportunities to build value in the new vehicle, and in yourself. *You only have one opportunity to make a great first impression, but you will have several opportunities to make additional great impressions. Remember, the more of an impression you make on your Customer, the more likely you are to make the sale.*

This has been a hotly debated topic for me in the past; If you have a Customer who expresses interest in a vehicle that you know is a piece of shit, do your best to steer them away from that vehicle. Why? Who is the first person that your Customer will call when they start having problems with that vehicle? YOU. They'll act like you built it yourself, and that you intentionally sold them a lemon. If you want to create Assets, don't sell people vehicles that you know are piles of garbage. They will appreciate the fact that you helped them to avoid stepping on a land mine. Sell them something else.

Anytime you have a Customer who expresses interest in viewing the inside of a vehicle, or preferably taking it for a test drive, here's what you should do next to keep building momentum. "Absolutely, I'll be right back" then hustle to the showroom, grab the keys and your plate, and hustle back out to the Customer. "Why do I have to hustle? Why can't I just walk normal, bro?" When your Customer sees you hustling on their behalf, it makes an impression on them. They like that. You aren't making them wait twenty minutes.

When you get back to the vehicle, pull it out into the open whenever possible. This separates the specific vehicle that your Customer is interested in from the other 30 vehicles in the row that they aren't particularly interested in. Now it's standing alone. This is when the Customer begins to develop mental ownership and an emotional attachment to that vehicle. During the walk around and test drive, you are going to build that mental ownership and emotional attachment as much as you can.

Start your walk around at the window sticker whenever possible. Hopefully, you saw your Customer pull into your lot with their old vehicle, but even if you didn't, ask them what kind of vehicle they are driving now *before* you begin your walk around. Why is this valuable information to know *before* you do your walk around? If you know what their old vehicle is, you will have a pretty good idea of what features to point out on the new vehicle that you're pretty sure their old vehicle doesn't have.

I want you to picture a stack. This stack is made up of hot buttons. The more hot buttons that you strike with your Customer, the more value you are building in the vehicle that they are interested in. And the more value you build in that vehicle, the more likely they are to want to take that vehicle home with them.

You don't need to read the entire window sticker to your Customer. It will take you thirty minutes, and it gets really freaking boring. Just point out the features that are hot buttons for most people, because if they are hot buttons for most people, they probably will be for your new Customer, as well. *Definitely point out the cool shit on the new vehicle that you're pretty sure their old vehicle does not have. Many of these will be hot buttons. Stack em' up!*

Starting at the window sticker, work counter-clockwise. Open up the back door so your Customer can see how roomy the back seat is. Fold the back seat down whenever possible, so when you open the trunk, the Customer will be able to see right into the passenger cabin. Cargo space is important to a lot of people. Continue to work counter-clockwise, and end the walk around at the driver's seat. Then, plant your Customer's butt right behind the steering wheel. (Don't actually touch your Customer's butt) **Way too many Salespeople skip this next step, and it costs them Car Deals and Money.** No matter how much your Customer likes the looks and features of this new vehicle, if they aren't comfortable in it, none of that other stuff matters. They may not be aware of the plethora of adjustments available to them so that they can get comfortable in the driver's seat. Therefore, take thirty seconds to make sure they are comfortable *before* you even think about taking your Customer out on a test drive.

Once the Customer is comfortable, it's time to hit the road. We were supposed to use a pre-determined test drive route with all of our Customers, but I let my Customers take the new vehicle wherever they saw fit. The test drive *is not* your time to be a chatterbox. You don't want to be a distraction to your Customer as they are driving this unfamiliar vehicle, and you want them to *experience* the vehicle. They might very well be picturing themselves showing off their shiny new car to their coworkers, their neighbors, their Family, etc. That mental ownership and emotional attachment to this new vehicle are further building. If they ask you a question about the vehicle while on the test drive, answer it thoroughly, then go back to being quiet. If they start asking you *personal questions*, this is a great sign. This means they like you enough to want to learn more about you, personally. **Customers buy cars from Salespeople who they like!**

When we returned from our test drives, we were supposed to ask the Customer "should we park this in the sold row while we go inside and button this up?" I tried it a couple of times when I was brand new to the Car Business, and it sucked. It made the Customer really uncomfortable, and it made me really uncomfortable. I heard things like "Seth, I don't even know what my trade is worth yet…" or "Seth, I don't even know what the payments are yet…" It was embarrassing, so I stopped doing it after a couple of horrifying attempts.

Remember, using this approach, at no point are you going to intentionally make your Customer uncomfortable. You are going to keep them as comfortable and happy as possible from first contact, all the way through delivery, and beyond. As a result, you'll sell more cars, and make a lot more Cash.

*In the interest of full disclosure, I *did not* go on every single test drive. I do not believe it is necessary to go on every test drive (I've sold over a thousand vehicles having not gone on the test drive.) There are cases when it is not in your best interest to go on the test drive (like when you have three or four Customers all at the same time.) And, there are cases when it isn't in your Customer's best interest for you to go with them on the test drive (like when a young girl wants to test drive a vehicle, but she clearly isn't comfortable with having a stranger accompany her on the test drive.) However, you *should* go on the test drive whenever possible. It gives you an opportunity to answer questions when they pop up, which they probably will. It also gives you an opportunity to further build rapport with your Customer.

If your Dealership has a strict policy that states that you must go on every single test drive, without exception, please just go on every single test drive. I want to help you sell more cars and make more Money; I have zero interest in getting you into trouble.

CHAPTER 4

After The Test Drive

Successful People Are Simply
Those With Success Habits
-Brian Tracy

There are quite a few different scenarios that can play out when you return from the test drive, the most desirable being "I'll take it!" That also happens to be the least likely scenario, but it does happen on occasion! When it does, it makes your whole day. You start looking at New Mansions on your local Real Estate website, you start checking out $150,000 Exotic Cars online, etc.

Ok, let's discuss the most common scenarios that will play out after the test drive.

If the Customer likes the vehicle, and they like you, the most common scenario will be "let's see what you can do." In that case, just say "excellent, follow me," then start walking toward the showroom. Most of the time the Customer will be two or three paces behind you, but it's never a bad idea to glance back just to make sure that they are, in fact, following you. Either show your Customer your Service Department or don't, depending on your Dealerships policy. Then, take the Customer to your desk.

Another common scenario is "This is my first stop. I still have three or four other vehicles to look at before I make my decision." In a case like that, always try to get the Customer's contact information before they leave your Dealership so that you can keep in touch with them. The best way to ask for a Customer's contact information is "Susan, what's the *best* number to reach you at?" vs. "Susan, what's your phone number?" What's the difference? Many people still have a landline (home phone) which also happens to be the phone number that you are least likely to reach them on. If you just ask them what their phone number is, this is often the first number that comes to their mind. But, when you ask them what the *best* phone number is to reach them on, their mobile number is usually the first number that comes to their mind. And their mobile phone is the one that you are most likely to reach them on. There is an entire Chapter dedicated to Follow Up later in this book.

One response that I used to get fairly often was "I need to bring my Husband/Wife back with me before I move forward." In that case, try to pencil in an appointment when they can come back to look at the vehicle together. If your Customer doesn't know when their Spouse is going to be able to make it back with them to view the vehicle, get their contact information so you can pencil in an appointment over the phone. Always get the contact information so you can Follow Up with the Customer.

Another fairly common scenario is "I'm on my lunch break. I can stop back after work; I can stop back Thursday, etc." Again, try to pencil in an appointment for when the Customer can make it back to move forward, and *get their contact information.* I'm going to drill this into your head throughout this book. ***The contact information is often the bridge that will allow you to transport your Customer from "Prospect" to "Owner."***

A scenario that used to crack me up was "this car rides too stiff/there's too much road noise/the seats are uncomfortable, etc." Then twenty minutes later that same Customer would purchase the same vehicle in a different color as if it was a completely different model. ***Remember, perception is reality. If the Customer thinks this vehicle rides better because it's a different color, it rides better because it's a different color.***

One scenario that used to really perplex me was the guy who started looking at new cars six months before his current lease was up. Why the hell are you looking at cars now? Your lease won't be up until we have the ability to land men on Pluto. Still, I would get their contact information so I could keep in touch with them periodically. Once a month or so.

There are many other scenarios that car play out when you return from the test drive, but these are definitely the most common. At least in my experience.

CHAPTER 5

Working The Deal

*Instead Of Thinking Outside The
Box, Get Rid Of The Box
-Deepak Chopra*

"Work the Customer, not the Sales Manager!" "God, you're a pain in the ass!" If I had a nickel for every time I heard those words, I'd have a boat-load of nickels. I never saw the point in only working the Customer. If I worked the Customer *and* the Sales Manager, wouldn't that increase my odds of selling a car? Yep. So, I worked them *both*. My Sales Managers may have thought I was a pain in the ass, but they sure didn't seem to mind when I walked into their offices over and over again with signed purchase orders...

In this Chapter, I am going to teach you how to be a relentless, tenacious, fiercely competitive pain in the ass. From now on, you will fight tooth and nail for every single Car Deal, regardless of what you are going to make on it. I've worked with guys who wouldn't even sell someone a car if they couldn't make at least a four or five-hundred-dollar commission on them. This never made any sense to me. They would spend three or four hours with a Customer, then send them packing if they couldn't make a big commission on them. You'd rather work for free than to at least make a couple hundred bucks? That is the dumbest shit I've ever seen. Don't do that. How much Money do you make when you lose your Customer to your competition? Does your competition send you a fifty-dollar referral check? Nope. If you lose your Customer to your competition, you make zero dollars.

Grab a sticky note. I'm only going to ask you to write two words on it. The first word is "Volume." What is the standard unit of measurement for success in the Car Business? Volume. Who gets "Salesperson of the Month" at your Dealership? The Salesperson who sells the most vehicles, right? Volume. Volume is without question your number one ticket to success in the Car Business. Most Dealerships have a generous Volume Bonus Pay Plan $$$.

The second word that I want you to write on your sticky note is "Service." What the hell does that mean? You are going to give *every* Customer a Buying Experience that is better than anything that they've experienced with any other Salesperson before meeting *you*. You are going to provide them with a service that makes them *want* to do business with you. There will be no need to try to force them to do business with you. Now, put that sticky note on your desk, or someplace where you will see it all the time. This will serve as a constant reminder to always keep those two words in mind. Taking on a Volume/Service mindset can dramatically transform your Career, as well as your Checking Account.

The first thing to do when you get your Customer back to your desk is to make sure that they are comfortable. Offer them a soda, a bottle of water, a cup of coffee, a beer, etc. And it's important that you go get it yourself. This is the part of the Buying Process when many Customers tense up because they are accustomed to dealing with high-pressure Salespeople. You want to make them as comfortable and relaxed as possible just before working the deal. Now, if you know that this Customer has already visited two or three other Dealerships before visiting yours, make your Sales Manager aware of it right up front. Hopefully, your Sales Manager has enough common sense to give you a strong number on the first pencil. It's pretty embarrassing to present numbers to a Fresh Customer that are five thousand dollars higher than the Dealership that they just left.

My Dealership used a four square style worksheet, which is designed to have the Customer point at the objection(s) if there are any. This is how I used to present the numbers to my Customers. I'd walk into my office and say "good news!" or "great news!" before I presented the numbers. This sets the expectation before you even tell them what the numbers are. Everybody loves good news! With a pen in hand, I would say, "Susan, the sale price on your new car is $20,995, your trade allowance is $10,000, so with $0 down, your payments are $350 for 60 months, $320 for 66 months, or $290 for 72 months. With my pen left on the worksheet, pointed at the lowest payment, I would ask, "which one of those sounds best to you?"

A couple of things that I'd like to point out; Every State has different tax laws regarding trade-ins. In New York, we have an 8% sales tax. But, any Customer who registers their new vehicle in NY only pays sales tax on the trade difference. So, in the example above, Susan would only pay sales tax on $10,995. In other words, she's saving $800 on sales tax simply because she's trading in a $10,000 vehicle. *If the State that your Customer is going to register their new vehicle in has a similar tax law, be sure to point this out to every Customer. Most Customers are unaware of this. It's a helluva pleasant surprise when they find out that they are going to save $800 on sales tax just by trading in their old vehicle.* Secondly, I always liked to give my Customers three payment options. This paints a perfect scenario for payment buyers. Often, they will point to the payment that best fits their budget, and you'll sell a car without giving up a nickel of gross.

Back to the deal with Susan. Let's say she points at the sale price and says "I can buy the same car at XYZ Motors for $19,995." This is where you ask for a commitment, "Susan, if I can talk my Manager down to $19,995, can we button this up for you today?" In most cases, she will say "yes." Susan likes you, and she obviously likes the vehicle or she wouldn't be sitting here working a deal on it with you. Anytime you have to go back to your Manager to ask for more Money, make it seem to your Customer like it's going to be a tall order. This gives them the perception that you are about to go fight for them. After Susan agrees to purchase the vehicle from you for $19,995, say, "Ok, wish me luck!" Then walk into your Manager's office.

This is where working your Sales Manager comes into play. Sit in front of your Sales Manager and say with a sigh "Here's the deal. She can buy the same car at XYZ Motors for $19,995. If we don't match their price, she's going to go buy the car there." With a frustrated tone ask, "what do you want to do?" That's not exactly what Susan said, but you don't want to lose her to your competition, right?? More often than not, your Sales Manager is going to want you to "bump" Susan. He'll probably agree to split it with her. Splitting the offer with the Customer is extremely common in the Car Business. He might say, "Tell her I'll split it with her. I'll do $20,495" Go back to your office and say "Good news! I couldn't get him all the way down to $19,995, but I did get a big concession. He agreed to come down to $20,495. How does that sound?" Don't be surprised when Susan thinks about it for a moment, and then says, "Ok, let's write it up!"

Why on Earth did Susan just agree to pay you $500 more than what she knows she can buy the same car at XYZ Motors for? Could it be because you provided her with such an outstanding Buying Experience? Could it be because you fought *for* her, instead of *with* her? Could it be because she has never dealt with a Salesperson who made the whole process so easy, before? On all counts, YES. This is the kind of thing you can expect on a daily basis when using The Full Circle Sales Approach. Get used to it.

Alright, let's say Susan points at her trade value as the objection and says "$10,000 is not enough for my trade. I looked it up online, and the website says it's worth $12,000" Then she pulls out the sheet to prove that her trade is, in fact, worth $12,000. Happens all the time. The number one mistake people make when they input their vehicle information into this website is they overstate the condition of their trade in. Everybody thinks their vehicle is in "Excellent" condition. They don't bother to read the definition of excellent condition. In this situation, ask Susan if you can take a look at her sheet and say "Wow, my Used Car Manager isn't usually that far off." Then, proceed to read her the definition of "Excellent," periodically looking up at her to verify that her vehicle matches this description. In most cases, the Customer's vehicle does not meet the criteria to meet these standards.

At no point during this process are you going to intentionally make your Customer feel stupid or insult them, unless you enjoy working for free.

More often than not, Susan is going to say "Well, it does have a big scrape on the front bumper, the check engine light is on, and my mechanic says it's going to need new tires, soon. Maybe it's not quite in "excellent" condition, but I need to get at least $11,000 for it." Again, you ask for a commitment. "Susan, if I can get you $11,000 for your trade, can we button this up for you today?" Susan will probably say "yes." Then you say, "Ok, wish me luck!" Walk into your Sales Managers office, sit down in front of him and say with a sigh "Here's the deal. She wants $11,000 for her trade or she's going to go buy a car at XYZ Motors. What do you want to do?" That's not exactly what Susan said, but you don't want to lose her to your competition, do you?? Your Manager will probably split the offer then tell you to get out of his office. Walk back into your office and say "Good news! I couldn't quite get $11,000 for your trade, but he did agree to split it with us. I got you $10,500, so now you're saving $840 on sales tax. That's like selling your car from your front yard for $11,340! What do you say we button this up?" Susan's either going to say "yes," or she's going to ask you to throw in mud guards, a cargo net, etc. You are so close to making a Car Deal! One way or another, Susan is getting those mud guards, a cargo net, or whatever!

I have used vehicle accessories many, many times over the years as a closing tool. But, I never paid for them, myself. I would never lose a Car Deal over a couple hundred bucks, and my Managers knew it. So, I wouldn't leave their office until they agreed to throw them in to make the deal. I was relentless, and you should be, too. Mudguards, cargo nets, remote start systems, trailer hitches, all weather floor mats, roof rack cross rails, etc. You name it, if it's a vehicle accessory, you can use it as a closing tool. If your Customer wants you to "throw it in" to close the deal. Don't leave your Manager's office until he agrees to throw it in, or at the very least, give the accessory or accessories to your Customer at "cost."

Now, let's say Susan points to the payment as the objection. Payment Buyers are my favorite. They are the easiest to close. Susan points at the 60-month payment and says, "I never finance for longer than 60 months, but $350 a month is way too high. My budget is $300 a month." Take a look at the worksheet, and say, "I understand. Susan, we deal with many different Banks, none of which charge a pre-payment penalty. So, you can finance the car for 66 months to lower your payment to $320 a month, then just pay a little extra whenever you're having a good month, financially. That way you will shorten the term, and *save yourself money* on interest." *(None of the Banks we dealt with charged a pre-payment penalty, so I used this line with Customers all the time. If the Banks that your Dealership does business with have the same setup, use this line as a closing tool.)* $320 a month for 66 months is higher than her stated budget, but it's $30 a month lower than the 60-month payment. It's a happy medium. Don't be surprised when Susan agrees to these terms. Now, you've sold Susan a vehicle without giving up any gross. This is why I love payment buyers.

Lease Customers tend to have a slightly different mindset. They almost *expect* to have to put Money down. This expectation can be used to your advantage. Let's say you work a Lease Deal with Susan. "Susan, good news! With $2,000 down your lease payment is $330 a month for 36 months, 12,000 miles per year. How does that sound?" She might say, "$330 a month is too high; I can't go over $300 a month." I would then educate Susan on what an additional $1,000 down will do to her payment on a 36-month lease. "Susan, this is only a 36-month lease, so if you put an extra $1,000 down, it will lower your payment by $28 a month. Then you'd be at $302 a month, and I'll go fight with my Manager to get you down to $300 a month, even. How does that sound?" Customers don't think the same way we do, so when you educate them on something like this, it might come as a pleasant surprise to them. Many times, your Lease Customer will respond with "Oh, I didn't know that. I can put an extra $1,000 down. Go see if you can get my payment down to $300 a month, even. If you can, I'll take it!" $2 a month on a lease is like $75. You aren't leaving your Sales Managers office until that payment is an even $300 a month.

Why do we go to such great lengths to get the Customer exactly what they want? Several reasons.

1. *It's much more likely that this Customer will turn into a Customer for life, an Asset.*

2. *It's much more likely that this Customer will give you a perfect Survey Score. (We'll discuss how to ask for a perfect survey later in this book.)*

3. *This Customer is going to tell a shit load of people how wonderful you are.*

Everybody wants to buy a car from a Salesperson like you when you go the extra mile to make sure the Customer gets exactly what they want. You have gone the extra mile to make sure that they were truly happy with their purchase. Remember, perception is reality for these people. If they think they got a great deal, they got a great deal. Capitalize on this every chance you get!

This was my favorite closing question for Customers who didn't feel comfortable disclosing whatever was holding them back from making the purchase; "Susan, I have to ask, it's part of my job…is there anything within reason we can do to button this up for you today?" This is a very low pressure, low key way to unearth whatever might be holding the Customer back from buying a car today. Pay close attention to the way it's worded. "Susan, I have to ask, it's part of my job" You are just doing your job. Often times the Customer will empathize with you after hearing those words. "Is there anything *within reason* we can do to button this up for you today?" The words "within reason" are thrown in to avoid having the Customer make you an unrealistic offer. This is a great closing question. I used it all the time, and it worked like a charm. Give it a try!

How about a bass-ackwards close that I can almost guarantee you've never heard, before? If I had done everything that I could possibly do to sell someone a car, but we were still $25 or $30 a month apart...and I could tell the Customer reeaaaally wanted the vehicle. They were just on the fence about pulling the trigger because it was slightly more than they could afford. At a moment when most Salespeople would turn up the pressure in an effort to get the Customer to sign on the dotted line *right now*, I would do *the exact opposite*. "Susan, I understand this is a big investment, and I understand that you are on a tight budget. I've been there myself. Listen, why don't you go home and sleep on it tonight, and give me a call in the morning to let me know what you'd like to do. If you want the car, I'll put a hold tag on it until we can get together to button up the paperwork. How does that sound?" No exaggeration, 90% of the time when I used that line, I would come into work the following morning, and the voicemail light on my phone would be blinking. "Hi Seth, this is Susan from last night. I thought it over, and I definitely want the car. Please put a hold tag on it and I'll stop in when I get out of work so we can do the paperwork." It was amazing. It worked so well; it was ridiculous. Probably because I had done the *opposite* of what the Customer expected me to do. The *opposite* of what most Salespeople do in that situation. I had pleasantly caught Susan off guard, and she appreciated it. Try it!

When you possess the ability to view the Buying Process from your Customer's point of view, as well as from your own perspective, you have an incredible advantage over every Salesperson who doesn't possess that ability. Many Salespeople simply don't care to look at things from their Customer's perspective. Little do they know that they are costing themselves Car Deals, and a lot of Money.

Look, I know not every Car Deal is going to easily come together. Some Customers are just super unrealistic about what they want to accomplish. I get it. Sometimes you'll need to get really creative to put a deal together. Extend the term, switch to a less expensive vehicle, switch to a lease, get a larger down payment from the Customer, bump the trade value, lower the price more, drop the interest rate, etc. There are many, many ways to skin this cat. From now on, it's your job to think of every possible way to put every Car Deal together. Don't rely on your Sales Manager to do it. If you have to, write a list of every possible option to put a Deal together, and check off every single option with every single Car Deal that you are having difficulty putting together. Here's an example list;

1. *Extend The Term*

2. *Switch To A Less Expensive Vehicle*

3. *Switch To A Lease*

4. *Bump The Trade Value*

5. *Lower The Price More*

6. *Get A Larger Down Payment*

7. *Lower The Interest Rate*

8. *See If Your Customer Qualifies For Any Additional Incentives; Military, Owner Loyalty, College Grad, Competitive Owner, Farm Bureau, Etc.*

9. *If Necessary, See If Your Customer Can Obtain A Strong Co-Signer*

10. *If The Co-Applicant Has Stronger Credit Than The Primary, Sometimes You Have To Make The Co-Applicant The Primary To Get The Deal Approved*

Any one of the above examples can lead to additional Car Deals EVERY month for you. Don't throw in the towel until you've checked off EVERY possibility on this list with EVERY Customer. Don't let any Car Deals slip through the cracks because you gave up too soon, without exploring EVERY possibility. You don't work for free! This will play a major role in increasing your Closing Ratio. A couple of things I'd like to point out. I was *not* a big fan of bagging trades, especially if I knew my Customer was getting quotes from several different Dealerships. My Sales Managers were aware of this, so they rarely bagged the trade on my Customers. We were not a one-price Dealership, so bagging the trade was not necessary to holding a strong gross.

Secondly, *don't get greedy.* There had been several times throughout my Career in the Car Business when I got greedy, and it almost always cost me a Car Deal. I wanted to hold a big gross on a certain Customer, so I gave them a price and stood my ground. When they asked me, "is that the best you can do?" I said, "yes it is." They would tell me that they had to talk it over with their Spouse, pray about it, consult with their Tarot Cards, etc. and that they would call me later. They'd call me later, but it usually wasn't with good news. They were calling to tell me that they had purchased a vehicle from my competition.

So, as a direct result of my greed, instead of making a $500-$600 commission, I made a $0 commission. It sucks ass to spend two or three hours with a Customer and have them buy a vehicle from your competition because you insist on making a large gross on them. In hindsight, I would have gladly taken a $200 commission over a $0 commission.

Your job is to sell the vehicle. Let your Management Staff worry about how much Money is being made on your Car Deals. Just sell as many vehicles as possible. Focus on Volume and Service, and let the rest sort itself out. Your Finance Manager will get a crack at every Customer that you sell a vehicle to, in an effort to generate additional revenue for your Dealership.

CHAPTER 6

F&I

What You Do Today Can
Improve All Your Tomorrows
-Ralph Marston

When I was 20 years old, brand new in the Car Business, my first Mentor was also my first F&I Manager. His name was Greg, and he was freaking awesome. I owe a lot of my success in the Car Business to Greg. He taught me a lot about selling cars, and definitely played a role in helping me to hit the ground running in this business. He also happens to be one of the funniest people that I've ever met. We used to love watching him do T.O.'s. He would make goofy faces at the Customers sitting across the desk from him when they weren't looking, then quickly go back to an "I'm totally paying attention to you" face when they looked back at him. It was hilarious. I've never met anyone with better comedic timing.

But, what really made Greg great was his uncanny ability to solidify Car Deals for us. Not only did he generate additional revenue for the Dealership, but he also turned shaky Customers into rock-solid Buyers. It was amazing. If I had any trepidation about whether or not a Customer that I had just written up was actually going to show up to take delivery of their new car, it was short lived. When I saw that Customer walk out of Greg's office laughing up a storm, I *knew* they were going to show up to take delivery of their new car. In my opinion, a great Finance Manager generates additional revenue for the Dealership by selling Extended Warranties, Paint Protection, etc. But, they also serve to solidify every Car Deal.

Look, I know that not every Finance Manager is created equal. I've worked with a few that I wanted to punch in the face on a regular basis. However, it is *definitely* in your best interest to stay on their good side whenever possible. There will come a time when you need them to do you a favor, or you'll need them to help you out of a jamb. They are much more likely to do so if you are on their good side. Example; You write a Customer up who has marginal credit, and you need your Finance Manager to pull some strings to get your Customer approved. Or, you need your Finance Manager to lower the interest rate a little bit to get your Customer's payment right where it needs to be so that you can deliver the car. You see? At some point, you will need your Finance Manager to be in your corner.

How do you go about staying on your Finance Managers good side? You can start by doing a proper T.O. with every Sold Customer. Your turnover to the Finance Manager does not need to be a twenty-minute ordeal. Here's how I used to do it, "Susan, thank you so much for your business. You made a great choice. What I'm going to do now is turn you over to Greg. Greg is going to go over your DMV paperwork with you; he's also going to discuss your warranty options with you. He has some other great things to share with you, as well. Greg will take great care of you. Susan, thank you again for your business, and I'll see you when you come to pick up your new car!" That's it, nothing spectacular.

Remember, Susan knows you, likes you, and trusts you. Otherwise, she would not have just spent a small fortune purchasing a vehicle from you. So, when you make the suggestion that your Finance Manager has some great things to share with her, and that he is going to take great care of her, she will be much more likely to pay attention to what he has to present to her.

Also, a little positive reinforcement goes a long way. We love it when out Bosses tell us "Great Job!" If your Finance Manager gets your Customer with marginal credit approved, shake his (or her) hand, and tell them that they did a great job, and thank them. Being an F&I Manager is often a thankless job. Be the Salesperson who makes them feel appreciated. It will pay dividends for you, believe me.

Many Dealerships offer a financial incentive to the Salesperson if the Finance Manager sells your Customer aftermarket products, my Dealership did. Hopefully, yours does, too. If your Dealership rewards *you* in some way when your Finance Manager sells aftermarket products to your Customer, this is all the more reason to do a great T.O. As the Salesperson, you have a lot to do with how successful your Finance Manager is with your Customers. Keep that in mind.

CHAPTER 7

Delivery, And How To Ask For A Perfect Survey

*It's Hard To Beat A Person
Who Never Gives Up
-Babe Ruth*

There was one Salesperson at the Dealership where I worked who would take three hours to deliver every car. He would go over the paperwork in minute detail, then go over every single feature of his Customer's new vehicle before they left the Dealership. There's no freaking way these poor people could retain that much information. It was just a huge waste of time. My deliveries lasted 45 minutes to an hour from A to Z. Anything more than that is just overkill.

When your Customer arrives to pick up their new car, this is a big occasion for them! Make it fun and exciting! Most Customers will probably want to do the paperwork before you show them the features of their new vehicle. Some people will want to view the vehicle first. It doesn't matter. Either way, you're still going to do the same stuff.

When you go through the paperwork with your Customer, go over it with them thoroughly, but don't read everything line by line. It's tedious and unnecessary. Once you complete the paperwork, this is the first time you'll ask for a perfect survey. This is the exact word track that I used with *every single* New Car Customer, and it worked very, very well.

(It is imperative that you take all the other steps laid out in this book up until this point to ensure that you get a great survey.)

"Susan, thank you so much for your business, I really appreciate it. You made a great choice; I know you'll love your new car. Listen, you're going to get a survey from the manufacturer. The survey is kind of like the car's report card, it's my report card, the Dealership's report card, etc. They will ask you a series of questions about your new car, about your Salesperson, about the Dealership, and about your overall experience with us. They ask you to grade each question from one to ten. One is horrific, and ten is good. This manufacturer is a very fast growing Company, and I'm sure they'd love to keep it that way, so they are super strict when they grade these surveys. It's tough for us, but they consider anything less than a ten to be "not good enough." If you could give me tens on everything, I'd REALLY appreciate it. (I'd give them a two thumbs up. Don't judge me, it works.) And, if you need anything, don't hesitate to give me a call or come visit me and I'd be happy to help you out!"

This is the *exact* word track that I used with every single New Car Customer, and it worked like magic. I consistently had some of the highest CSI Scores in our Region. I strongly encourage you to give it a try. Just remember, first you need to do all of the other things that we've discussed in this book leading up to delivery. We aren't done with this subject just yet.

If this Customer has never purchased a vehicle from your Dealership before, make sure you show them where to go for service before you take them out to view their new vehicle. It's pretty embarrassing when they come in for their first service, and they wander around your showroom like zombies because they don't know where to go. Take the two minutes to point out your Service Department to every new Customer.

Once you've completed the paperwork with your Customer, asked for a perfect survey, and pointed out your Service Department, now it's time to show them their new vehicle. Enthusiastically walk them out to their new vehicle, as if you are introducing them to their newborn baby. (Wow, that sounds corny as hell.) Then, begin to show them how the features of the vehicle operate. You don't need to show them *everything,* but definitely show them how to operate the features that they will use on a daily basis. Headlights, windshield wipers, climate control, radio, tilt and telescoping steering wheel, cruise control, Bluetooth, seat adjustment, trunk opener, fuel door opener, etc. Also, if you know that certain features are going to be on the survey, make sure you cover them with your Customer for obvious reasons.

As I showed my Customers the climate control and radio, I would have them sit in the driver seat, and I would sit in the passenger seat. After showing them how to operate the major features of the vehicle, I would say, "Do you have any questions about the car before you leave?" "Not that I can think of." "Susan, thank you so much for your business. I know you are going to love the car. If you could take care of me with tens on the survey, I would really appreciate it." *Two thumbs up, again. I don't care if it looks dumb, it works.* "Again, if you have any questions about the car, please don't hesitate to call me, or just come visit me. I'd be happy to help you. By the way, if you know of anybody else who needs a new vehicle, send them my way! If you send me a Customer who ends up purchasing a vehicle, I'll send you a check for fifty bucks! It's an easy way to make a little extra money!" Then, I would send Susan on her way.

That's it! The delivery does not have to be a marathon. I asked Susan for a perfect survey on two separate occasions *and* asked her for referrals for the first time. In the next Chapter, we'll follow up with Susan, ask her for a perfect survey once again, and ask her for referrals again.

For a lot of Salespeople, the great service ends after the Customer takes delivery of their new car. That is a major mistake. If you want to create Customers for Life (Assets), the great service *never* ends. Remember, the more Assets that you have in your Community, the easier your job gets. A prominent Dealer Operations Manager once said to me "The longer you're in the Car Business, you should work less and make more." I couldn't agree more. Using this Approach, that is exactly what you will experience.

CHAPTER 8

Follow. Up.

Follow Up Two Or Three Times.
They'll Remember Your Name
When It's Time To Call Back
-Andrew Dornenburg

Follow up is such a huge part of this business. Sadly, far too many Salespeople lazily miss the boat on this one. You aren't going to be one of those Salespeople. In this Chapter, we'll discuss how to follow up with Customers who *have* already purchased a vehicle, as well as Customers who *have not* purchased a vehicle. Yet.

First, let's follow up with Susan. We used to have a strict three day follow up policy with our new Customers. Three or four days after delivery is about the sweet spot in my opinion. Here's how I would follow up with my new Customers. "Hi Susan, it's Seth from ABC Motors! I just wanted to touch base with you to see how everything is going with your new hot rod?" More often than not, you'll hear things like "Oh my God, I love it. I took it on a trip over the weekend and got 53.2 miles per gallon. This is the best car everrrrrr!"

Sometimes they'll have questions. Most of the time you can address their questions right over the phone. If you can't, invite them back to the Dealership so you can address the issue in person. Then, I'd ask for a perfect survey, once again. "Susan, thank you so much again for your business. If you would take care of me with tens on the survey, I'd greatly appreciate it! Again, if you know anyone who needs a vehicle, please send them my way."

This is a great way to follow up with a new Customer. You're covering all the bases. You're making sure they're happy with their new vehicle, answering any questions that they might have, asking for a perfect survey again, and asking for referrals again. After that original follow-up call, I'd only touch base with my Customers maybe twice a year. Calling them on their Birthday is an *awesome* way to score brownie points with your Customers. Keep in mind, these people like you, so they wouldn't mind hearing from you on occasion. Taking time out of your busy schedule to call them and wish them a Happy Birthday is a very pleasant surprise to them! The General Public is used to Salespeople who bounce around from Dealership to Dealership, so touching base with them a couple of times a year is a great way to make them aware that their favorite Salesperson hasn't moved on to a different Dealership.

Don't badger people. We used to have a "Business Development Center" where we were supposed to call our Owners to ask for referrals on a regular basis. It was very, very annoying and uncomfortable for the Salespeople *and* our Customers. "Who's the next one in your Family who is going to purchase a vehicle? What's their phone number? Is it ok if I call them?" I despised that shit, and so did the Customer. It didn't work. If you follow the steps laid out for you in this book, you'll get referrals without having to badger people. When your Customer hears of someone who needs a vehicle, you will be *the first* Salesperson that they think of. Badgering them is unnecessary and counterproductive.

Following up with people who *have not* purchased a vehicle from you yet is even more important. We already discussed how to ask for the Customer's *best contact information*. If I had a Customer come in before 2:00 or 3:00, I would follow up with them later that night. "Hi Susan, it's Seth from ABC Motors. I just wanted to touch base with you to thank you for your time today, and to see if you had any questions that I can answer for you before I head home tonight." If there is an underlying objection, you are much more likely to unearth it over the phone than you are when the Customer is sitting three feet from you. Customers tend to have "phone muscles" when they aren't looking you in the face. That's ok; you can't overcome an objection if you don't know what it is. Once you uncover the objection, invite the Customer back to the Dealership so you can gang up on your Sales Manager together. (I used that line with Customers all the time! They love hearing that you are going to battle your Sales Manager alongside them!)

If Susan came to the Dealership at night, I'd follow up with her the same exact way the following morning. The objective should always be to get the Customer back in the Dealership. However, I have closed a lot of Car Deals right over the phone. Especially if the Customer lived thirty or forty miles away. If your Customer likes your product, just find a way to put the deal together. I don't care of it's over the phone, in your showroom, or in the bathroom at the truck stop. Just sell the car.

Remember that guy who started looking at cars ages before his lease was up? Follow up with him once a month, just to keep yourself fresh in his mind. When he is finally ready to get a new vehicle, you want to be the first Salesperson that he thinks of. Hopefully, you aren't retired by then.

A fantastic reason to follow up with someone who hasn't purchased a vehicle yet is when your manufacturer comes out with an extra incentive on the vehicle that the Customer expressed interest in. Or, when your Dealership has a "Sale" or an end of the month promotion. Lest ye forget, people want to feel like they got a good deal. If they think they got a good deal, they got a good deal.

TAKE A LOT OF NOTES. Write everything down. Your appointments, your deliveries, Customers that you need to follow up with, etc. Then, review the notes that you've taken over the last couple of months, every single day! This is a super easy way to find an extra one or two Car Deals every month. If you encountered a

Customer a month ago who still hasn't purchased a vehicle, and now there's an extra $500 incentive that didn't exist the last time you spoke to them, call them! The next thing you know, they'll be sitting in front of you purchasing a vehicle. BOOM!

CHAPTER 9

Working The Service Department

The Best Revenge Is Massive Success
-Frank Sinatra

A while back, I was having a conversation with a General Sales Manager buddy of mine, who used to be one of my competitors. (He became a GSM, and I became an Automotive Sales Trainer. Different strokes for different folks, I guess.) We were talking about working the Service Department. He asked me if I used to work my Service Department. I thought about it for a few seconds, and replied, "No, I didn't." He was surprised. Then, after a few days, it struck me! Wait a minute, yes I did! I just did it differently from everybody else. (Starting to see a trend here?)

Throughout my thirteen years in the Car Business, there always seemed to be a thin layer of animosity between the Service and Sales Departments. It was like they saw us as the rich ones, cruising around in fancy cars, rubbing our untold riches in their faces. And we saw them as the ones who worked their fingers to the bone and drove around in fifteen-year-old rust buckets. What I did was to break down that invisible barrier.

I had no interest in hanging out in the Service Department's waiting room, asking random people if they'd like to look at a shiny new car. That wasn't my style. Instead, I made friends with the Service Writers, the Service Manager, the Technicians, the Parts Department Personnel, and even the Lot Personnel.

The Service Department Personnel spend their entire day surrounded by people who desperately need a new vehicle, and you want to be the first person that they refer these Customers to.

If you treat them right, all of these people can be Assets for you. They can all be referral sources, and many of them will purchase vehicles from you, themselves! I lost count a long time ago of all the referrals that I received from my coworkers, and you can do the same thing! Capitalize on your likability, your charisma, and your sense of humor with *everybody*, not just your Customers.

I used to get yelled at all the time for hanging out in the Service Department, goofing off, making people laugh, throwing the football around, breaking shit, etc. Those guys loved it! Therefore, I was often the first Salesperson who came to mind any time they heard of someone who needed a vehicle.

It's pretty freaking awesome when at least once or twice a month, you have a Service Customer wander into your showroom looking for you, because one of the Service Department Personnel referred that Customer to you. This Customer needs a new vehicle, and you're going to help them find one. This is an easy way to pick up an extra fifteen or twenty Car Deals a year. Or more!

Another *huge* reason to treat these people with respect is that there will come a time when you need them to do you a favor. Or, you will need them to bail you out of a jamb. For example, you forget to make the Service Department aware that your delivery needs a trailer hitch, and you remember an hour before your Customer is scheduled to come pick up their new car. You need the Service Department to bail you out! They are much more likely to do so if you treat them right. No? Or, you sell a car to someone who lives out of town, and they want to take it home with them in an hour. You need the Lot Personnel to bail you out! They need to do a good job cleaning up your Customer's new car, in part to ensure that you get a great survey. Offer to buy them lunch if you have to, you need that car to look awesome when you deliver it.

Moral of the story? Treat everybody with dignity and respect, whether they make $8 an hour, or $800 an hour. What comes around goes around. Not only will you create a bunch of new Assets, but you'll also create Allies who will bail you out of a jamb when the time comes.

The time WILL come when you need these people to help you out. Don't take them for granted, and don't treat them like they aren't as important as you are just because you make more Money than they do.

CHAPTER 10

Time Management

Time Is More Valuable Than Money.
You Can Get More Money, But
You Cannot Get More Time
-Jim Rohn

Take. Your. Day. Off. I've seen way too many people work sixty or seventy hours a week for their entire life, and then die unexpectedly. That is a fucking travesty. I do not want you to be one of those people. Using this Approach, you will sell plenty of cars, and make plenty of Money, without the need to put in a ridiculous amount of hours at work.

This was always a point of contention at my Dealership. Almost everyone that I worked with worked their day off. Many of them ended up divorced. Many of them ended up getting burned out. And, many of them ended up an alcoholic. I refused to work on my day off unless I absolutely had no other choice, and the Management Staff hated it. But, I didn't care. Life is too short to spend half of it at work. I sold plenty of cars without working that extra day every week. Therefore, I very rarely made an appearance at the Dealership on my days off.

Spending time with these two knuckleheads
was far more important to me.

In life, there is no rewind button. The moments that you miss with your Friends, your Family, your Kids, your Significant Other, etc. because you were stuck at work? You can never get those back. I am so grateful that I learned this at such a young age. Far too many people don't realize this until it's too late. Now, I am passing this knowledge on to you. Please don't let your Career take over your life. Balance can be difficult to find, but you will find it if you sincerely seek it. In the Car Business, you already spend a shit load of hours at work. You need time to decompress. To recharge your batteries. Take that time. You've earned it.

Sometimes, the only day your Customer can make it into your Dealership for an appointment, delivery, etc. is on your day off. I get it. In that case, you have no other choice. But, that *does not* mean that you have to spend the entire day at work. Sometimes, the last day of the month happens to fall on your day off. I get it. In that case, you might have to at least make an appearance for a couple of hours, or perhaps switch your day off.

Use your head when it comes to scheduling appointments, deliveries, etc. Don't schedule two appointments thirty minutes apart. Inevitably, both Customers will show up at the same time, and suddenly you're in a bind. Space your appointments far enough apart to create a cushion, because you know damn well that one Customer will show up an hour late, and the other Customer will show up an hour early. Hopefully, you have a buddy at the Dealership, who will help you out when you have two or more Customers show up at the same time. I know that a lot of Dealerships do "split deals." Remember, 50% of something is better than 100% of nothing. Would you rather have $50 or $0? That's what I thought.

CHAPTER 11

Positive Energy And The K.I.S.S. Principle

Simplicity Is The Key To Brilliance
-Bruce Lee

Have you been around someone who has the ability to light up a room, without uttering a word? Why does this happen? Is it because they are the most physically attractive person in the room? Is it because they are wearing fancy clothes or expensive jewelry? Probably not. There's just something about them that commands attention. It's like a magnet. *It's their energy.* These are the people who see the good in every situation. Surely, you know Salespeople like this.

On the flip side, we all know people who bitch, piss, and moan about anything and everything. These people are like a cancer. Spend enough time around them, and you'll begin to mirror their behavior. These are the people who see the bad in every situation. They are chock full of negative energy. At times, you can even feel the tension when you're around them. Surely, you know Salespeople like this.

Now, put yourself in your Customer's shoes. Which one of the above Salespeople would you rather do business with? The one who is ambitious, exuberant, and full of life? Or, the one who has poor body language, a bad attitude, and always seems to have a cloud over their head? You don't need to be a Brain Surgeon to figure that one out.

Distance yourself from negative influences, whether it be at your Dealership, on Social Media, wherever. Surround yourself with people who bring you up, and distance yourself from people who bring you down. Stay away from negative people at your Dealership. Unfollow friends on Social Media who keep your newsfeed full of negative crap. You can remain friends, but you won't see their constant "woe is me" status.' Find Social Media pages that inspire and motivate you, and follow them. Keep your newsfeed full of inspirational and motivational quotes, stories, and videos. It will make all the difference in the world.

Have fun at work! You spend an awful lot of time at your Dealership; you might as well have a little fun while you're there. I used to get yelled at on a daily basis. We used to play practical jokes on each other, drag race brand new cars, have punching contests (we would punch each other in the arm as hard as possible until one of us gave up), play football in the Service Department after hours, etc. It was a blast! And, it went a long way to keeping Company Morale on a high note. Incorporate things like that into your own Career, just don't get fired doing it.

The K.I.S.S. Principle is an acronym for Keep. It. Simple. Stupid. It was developed by the United States Military (Navy, I believe) in the early 1960's. In essence, it means don't overcomplicate things. *The shortest distance between two points is a straight line. The Full Circle Sales Approach Is A Straight Line.* You make a great first impression, showcase your likeability and charisma, and you remain consistent throughout the entire Buying Process. Overcomplicating anything in your professional or personal life makes it less efficient, and it's counterproductive.

I had a sticky note on my desk that had, "Keep. It. Simple. Seth." written on it to serve as a constant reminder to not overcomplicate things at work or home. (I was able to substitute "Stupid" for "Seth" because they both start with "S.") Of course, having a sticky note on your desk doesn't automatically mean that keeping things simple will just magically fall into place. You have to make a conscious effort to make it happen.

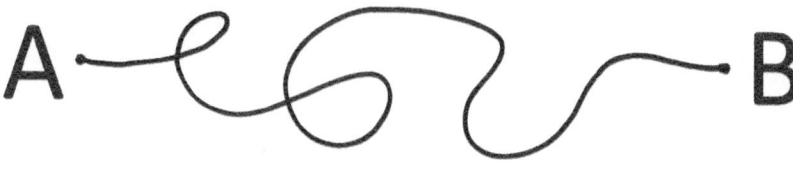

KEEP. IT. SIMPLE.

CHAPTER 12

Overview And Thank You!

*Whether You Think You Can, Or You
Think You Can't - You're Right
-Henry Ford*

Hopefully, now you have a strong grasp on what The Full Circle Sales Approach really is, and why it's so powerful. Especially compared to the outdated, "Old School, Always Be Closing" approach to the sale that's been a mainstay in the Automotive Industry for far too long. The average Closing Ratio in the Car Business is only 25% using that approach to the sale. It literally gets more and more counterproductive every year. Using The Full Circle Sales Approach, you should have little problem reaching a 50% Closing Ratio, or higher.

Giving every Customer an outstanding Buying Experience is more important now than in any other time in History. Now you know how to do it right the first time, every time. I strongly encourage you to keep this book in your desk at your Dealership. You can use it as a quick reference any time you get stuck with something, or to light a fire under your ass when things get slow. (Don't literally set the book on fire. Also, please don't actually set your ass on fire.)

***Let's do an overview of everything that
you've learned in this book.***

You learned how to take your goal setting to a whole new level, and how to harness the power of your subconscious mind to help make your dreams a reality. Just remember, simply writing your goals down is not enough. **You need to take Action.** If you take steps every day in the direction of your dreams, eventually you will reach them.

You learned the difference between Assets and Liabilities, and why it's so important to maximize the number of Assets in your Community. You also learned why it's so important to minimize the amount of Liabilities in your Community. Once you have a large amount of Assets in your Community, your Sales will be on Autopilot. That's a beautiful thing.

You learned how to leverage your likability, charisma, and sense of humor to make a great first impression on your lot, in your showroom, or over the phone. When you do this, your Customer will naturally get to know you, like you, and trust you. Add in a quality vehicle at a fair price, and you will be a freaking sales Ninja in no time. Remember always to hand every Fresh Customer your Business Card right up front! You also learned a few Jedi mind tricks, such as using the Customer's first name and asking them "yes questions" throughout the Buying Process, making it more likely that they will say *yes* to you when you ask them for the sale.

Aligning your interests with your Customer's interests is huge. Make them aware right up front that you are on their team, that you are their advocate, and that you will do everything in your power to help them find a vehicle that meets their wants, needs, and budget. Add to that the perception that you are going to fight to get them the best possible deal, and you'll be an unstoppable force. Don't forget to use the "it's the end of the month" mind hack to boost your end of the month sales.

"Just looking" is just a knee-jerk response that you now know how to get past by getting the Customer to start asking you questions. Once they start asking you questions, you've moved on to the next step in the process. Look at you go! Damn, you're going to be a Sales Master before you know it, strutting around with a $5,000 watch and driving a $50,000 sports car.

You also learned that you will have several opportunities to make a great impression on every Customer. The more of an impression you make on every Customer, the more likely you are to make the Sale. Customers don't want to do business with a Salesperson who is insincere, most of the time they can see right through it. So, be authentic and sincere. Make the entire Buying Process enjoyable.

You learned how to do a great walk around, and how to point out the features on the new car that you know their old car doesn't have, many of which will become hot buttons. The higher you build that stack of hot buttons, the more your Customer will desire to take that new car home with them. You now know how to subtly build that mental ownership and emotional attachment to the vehicle that your Customer is interested in. Getting every Customer's contact information is critical. Now you know the best way to ask for it.

There are several scenarios that can play out when you return from the test drive. Everything from, "let's see what you can do" to "I have six months left on my lease." Now you know exactly how to handle the most common scenarios.

You learned how to be a tenacious, relentless pain in the ass while working the deal! Work your Sales Manager even harder than you work your Customers! Fight for *every* Car Deal, regardless of what you are going to make on it. When your Customers see you fighting *for* them instead of *with* them, they will naturally *want* to buy a car from you. Volume is your key to success in the Car Business, don't allow anybody to hold you back! Release the brakes, and become the fiercely competitive freight train that you were born to be. You now have a list of things to check off with every single Customer before pulling the plug on any Car Deal. Use it! *Don't get greedy, just sell as many vehicles as possible.*

Staying on your Finance Managers good side is in your best interest. Now you know how to make that happen. Doing a proper T.O. is a great place to start. Showering them with positive reinforcement is also a good way to stay in their good graces. There will definitely come a time when you need your Finance Manager to bail you out.

Doing a thorough delivery is incredibly important, it makes you much more likely to get a great survey score. You have the exact, goofy ass word track that I used throughout my Career in the Car Business to maintain ridiculous CSI Scores. Take all of the steps that you've learned leading up to asking for a perfect survey, and you will be good to go the vast majority of the time. You will ask for a perfect survey twice during delivery, and ask for referrals at least once.

The importance of follow-up cannot possibly be overstated in the Car Business. Following up with your new Owners three or four days after delivery is another great time to ask for a perfect survey and referrals. Remember, your outstanding Customer Service *does not* come to an end as soon as your Customer leaves your lot in their new car. Following up with Customers who have not purchased from you yet is a no-brainer. Try to have some sort of perceived benefit for them whenever possible when you make a follow-up call. For example, "we're having an end of the month sale" or "the manufacturer just came out with an extra incentive" or, call to quiz them to see if they qualify for any special incentive programs.

Your Service Department is chock full of potential Assets for you! Start making friends with them now, and before you know it they'll start sending you referrals. Hell, any employee who isn't in Sales can become an Asset for you. Capitalize on this!

Take your day off. Time management is really important in the Car Business. You spend a shit load of time at your Dealership; you deserve to take some time for yourself, your Friends, your Family, etc. Life is way too short to spend half of it at work. Be sure to schedule a cushion between appointments and deliveries. Customers are notorious for *not* showing up on time.

Customers would much rather do business with a Salesperson who is ambitious and enthusiastic than a Salesperson who acts like their dog just died. It seems like this would be common sense, but apparently it isn't. I've seen far too many Salespeople who act like the World is going to come to an end at any given moment. Distance yourself from these negative Salespeople, and surround yourself with positive, inspirational, and motivational influences. Social Media can be a great source for motivation and inspiration.

The Full Circle Sales Approach is a systematic, actionable approach to the sale that also happens to be the most efficient and effective sales approach that I've ever seen. When you put all of the pieces of this puzzle together, it creates a masterpiece that your Customers will want to be a part of. Put these principles into Action, and you will transform into an unstoppable force of nature who will leave your competition in your wake. It's time to kick some ass.

I'd like to take this time to thank you, sincerely. It's Salespeople like you who make what I do rewarding and fulfilling. I love what I do, and I wouldn't be in this position without people like you. Again, thank you so much. Now, go sell some shit!

Action Is The Foundational
Key To All Success
-Pablo Picasso

www.ingramcontent.com/pod-product-compliance
Lightning Source LLC
Chambersburg PA
CBHW022131170526
45157CB00004B/1833